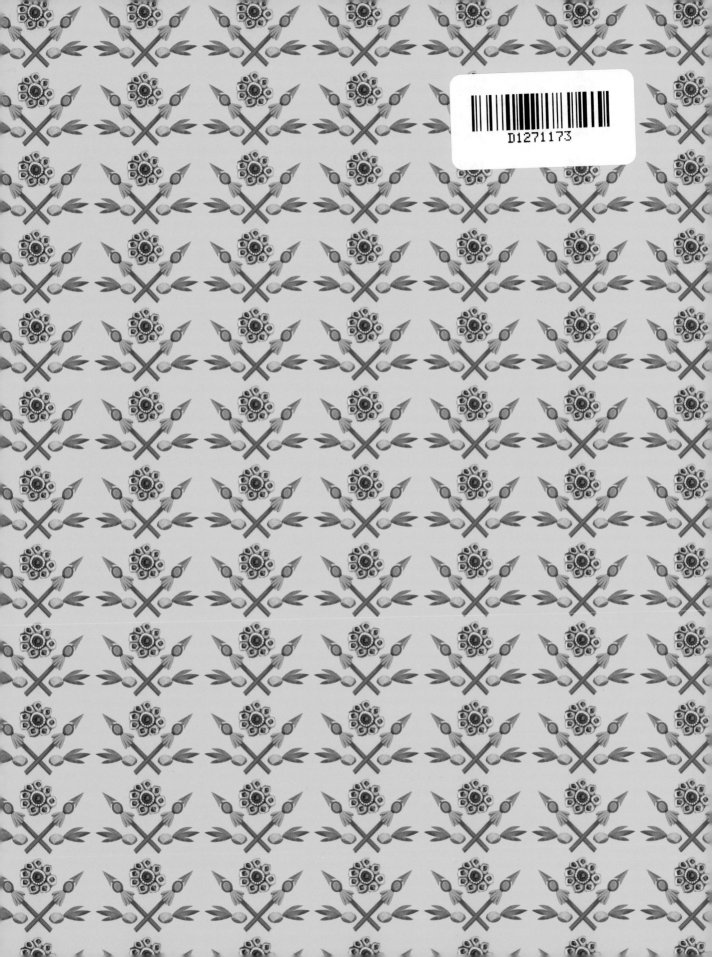

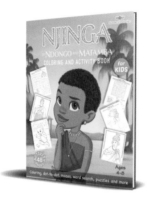

Register with us to receive a free digital copy of the "Njinga of dongo and Matamba" coloring and activity book.

bit.ly/NzingaCAB

OTHER BOOKS IN THE "OUR ANCESTORIES" LINEUP

THIS BOOK BELONGS TO:

Beth ♡

To The Lowry Family
♡
Happy Reading
Ekiuwa

ISBN: 978-1-7771179-5-5 (Hardcover)

First Print Edition.

www.our-ancestories.com

Our Ancestories

NJINGA
OF NDONGO AND MATAMBA

WRITTEN BY
EKIUWA AIRE

ILLUSTRATED BY
NATALIA POPOVA

Over 400 years ago, in what is now Angola, a baby girl was born. She was the daughter of the *soba* (the traditional ruler). He was called Mbandi Kiluanji, and he was of the Kimbundu people of Ndongo.

But something was wrong. During the baby's birth, her mother's cord became twisted around her neck. She was not breathing!

The nurse gently wrapped the baby in soft cloths and took her to the *soba*. "The baby is dying," she explained tearfully.

Taking the silent baby, *Soba* Kiluanji looked carefully into her tiny face. There was strength in her; he was sure of it. He did not want his daughter to die. He did not even know her yet, but already he loved her dearly. What could he do? *Perhaps I could breathe for her, he thought.*

Drawing a deep breath, the *soba* covered the baby's mouth and nose with his own mouth. Then he gently blew air into her lungs.

He looked again at her face. Still no crying. No breathing. But yet, he saw her strength. She wanted to live.

Taking another deep breath, he again carefully filled her lungs.

Again and again, *Soba* Kiluanji breathed for his daughter. He would not give up.

Finally, the baby cried ... and moved. She was alive!

The *soba* laughed with delight.

"I was certain she was lost, but you have breathed life back into her!" exclaimed the nurse.

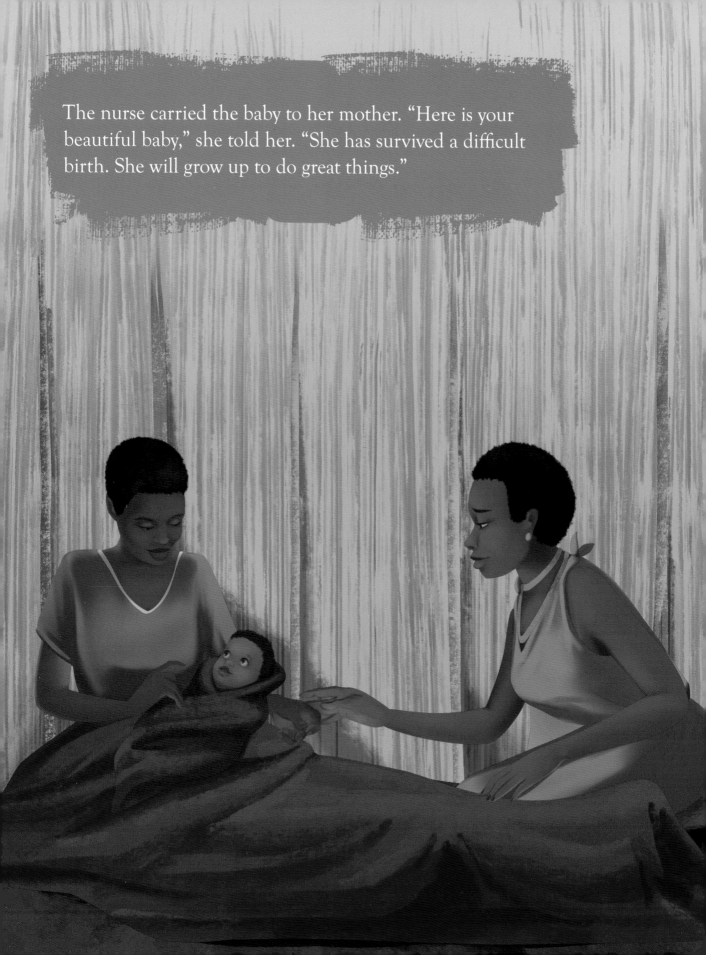

The nurse carried the baby to her mother. "Here is your beautiful baby," she told her. "She has survived a difficult birth. She will grow up to do great things."

The story of the ruler's exceptional daughter quickly spread.
Soon, it reached the ears of Mbandi, her *pangueami* (brother).

But what is so great about her? Mbandi
wondered. She was only a baby and not
even a boy! Everyone knew that the
firstborn son was the most important
child!

She is not special, he thought.

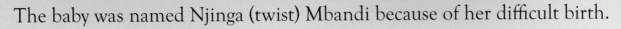

The baby was named Njinga (twist) Mbandi because of her difficult birth.

She was strong, healthy, active, and bright. She captured her father's heart from the very beginning. *Soba* Kiluanji loved to play with Njinga.

When she was old enough, he sent her to *xikola* (school) because he wanted her to learn to read and write in Portuguese. The Ndongo kingdom often had dealings with the government of the European country of Portugal.

Mbandi was not happy. "School is not for girls," he said.

The *soba* did not listen to him. "Your sister is quite smart," he said. "She will go to school with you."

One day, when Njinga was seven, her teacher (a Portuguese missionary) asked a question. "Do you know how to recite your numbers in Portuguese?"

"Of course," answered Njinga. "*Zero, um, dois, três...*"

Njinga kept going. Just as she passed the number twelve, Mbandi interrupted her.

"The teacher has only taught us up to the number ten," he said. "How do you know these other numbers?"

"I studied at home," answered Njinga. "I can go all the way to one hundred!"

The teacher laughed and later reported the story to the *soba*. "My, you are clever, Njinga," he said.

Mbandi scowled. *It isn't fair. She's just showing off! Njinga should not be allowed in school!*

A few years later, Njinga's father was crowned the *ngola* (king) of Ndongo. He started to invite Njinga to join him in attending to the business of the kingdom. This made Mbandi even more unhappy.

Njinga watched eagerly as her father went about his duties.

When she was old enough, the *ngola* even took Njinga to war. "Why do you bring her, Father?" asked Mbandi. "She can do nothing. She's a waste of time."

But *Ngola* Kiluanji disagreed. "As an infant, she fought to live. She is a fighter."

"I don't see anything special about her," objected Mbandi. "She's just a girl."

Njinga listened closely as her father talked with other rulers or made military plans. She learned everything she could. It became clear that she not only breathed her father's breath but also shared his talent for leadership. As time passed, Portugal made more rules for the people of the kingdom. *Ngola* Kiluanji fought back for many years.

The constant fighting made him very sad and *kuhoka* (tired).

In 1617, *Ngola* Mbandi Kiluanji joined the ancestors.

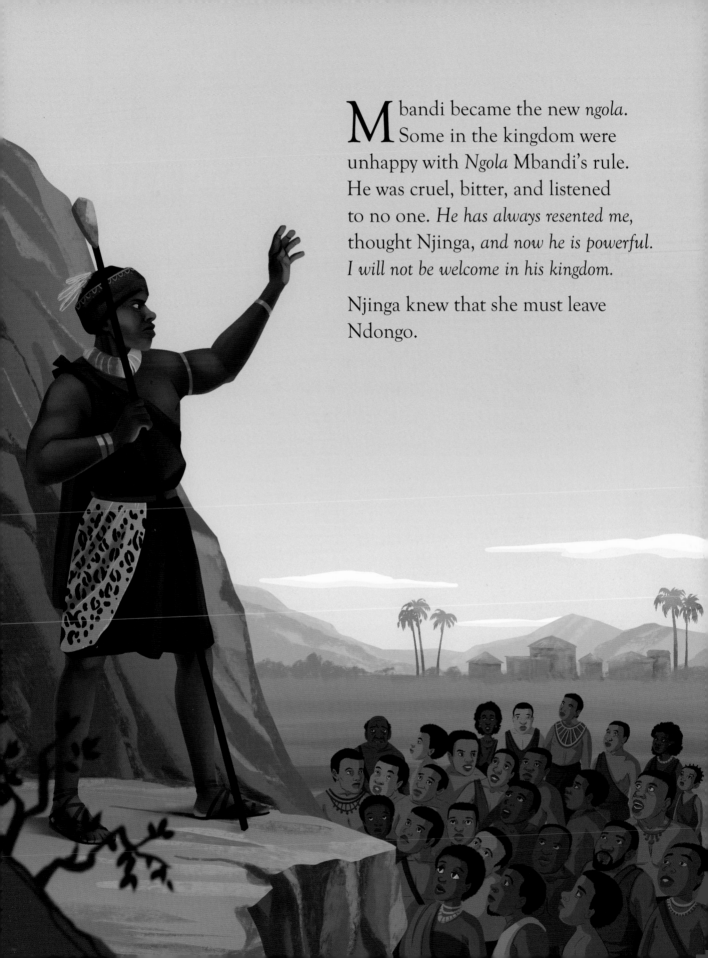

M bandi became the new *ngola*.
Some in the kingdom were
unhappy with *Ngola* Mbandi's rule.
He was cruel, bitter, and listened
to no one. *He has always resented me,*
thought Njinga, *and now he is powerful.*
I will not be welcome in his kingdom.

Njinga knew that she must leave
Ndongo.

Helped by her faithful *mukua-mbele* (helpers),
Njinga ran away to a nearby kingdom of Matamba.

Things did not go well for the Ndongo kingdom under *Ngola* Mbandi's rule. The Portuguese government threatened to take over, demanding riches and slaves from among the people.

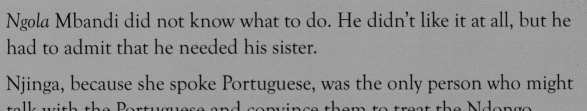

Ngola Mbandi did not know what to do. He didn't like it at all, but he had to admit that he needed his sister.

Njinga, because she spoke Portuguese, was the only person who might talk with the Portuguese and convince them to treat the Ndongo kingdom fairly. So, Mbandi swallowed his pride and sent for her.

Njinga did not trust her brother. *It may only be a trick so that he can hurt me*, she thought. But she knew that her people needed her help. Despite the danger, she decided to return.

Njinga went to Luanda, in the heart of the Ndongo kingdom, to see the Portuguese governor, Dom João Correia de Sousa. There, she expected to be treated as an equal.

But de Sousa sat in a grand chair and directed her to sit on the floor. This was to let everyone know that Njinga was not nearly as important as he was.

It did not work. When Njinga spoke to her *mukua-mbele* (helpers), one of them dropped down to his hands and knees, creating a proper chair for her. On his back, Njinga sat like a queen on her throne, looking the governor straight in the eyes.

Njinga's mission was a success! She outsmarted the Portuguese, convincing them to be kinder to her people.

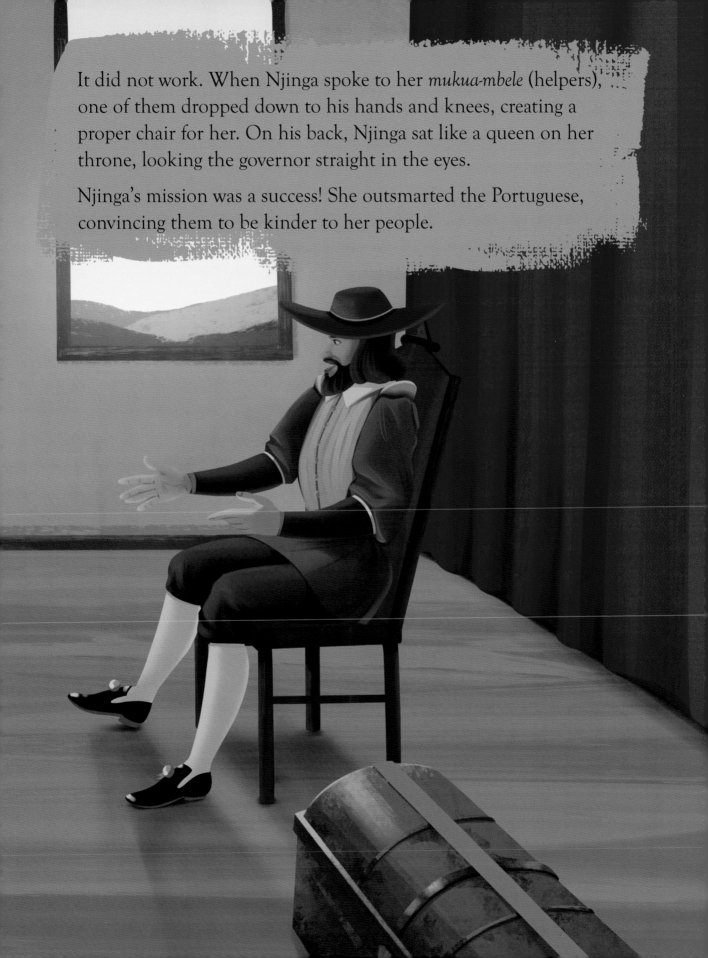

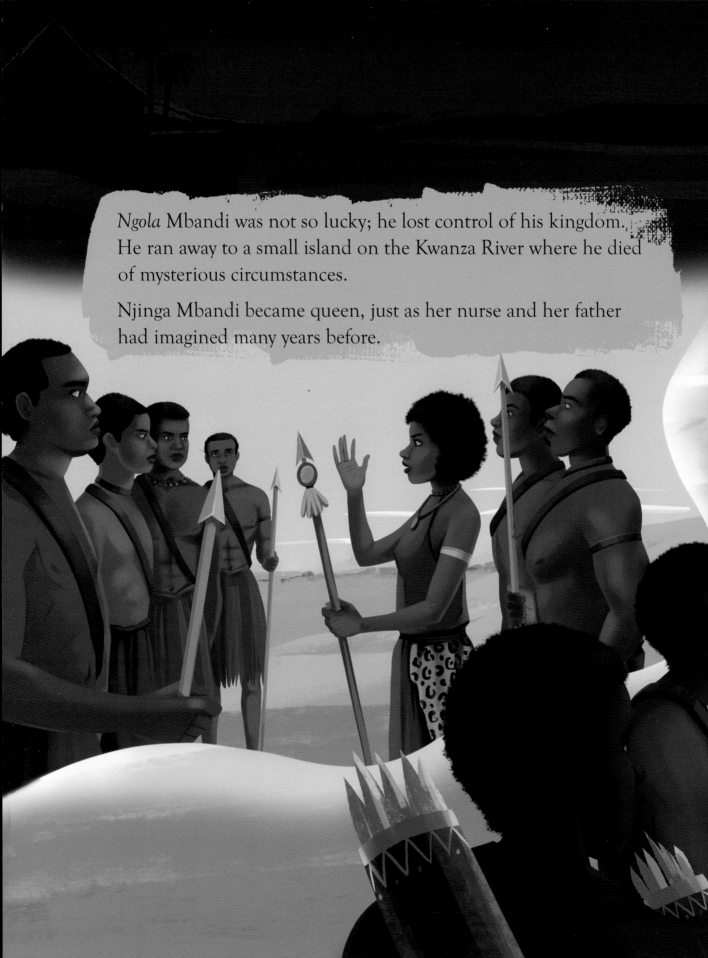

Ngola Mbandi was not so lucky; he lost control of his kingdom. He ran away to a small island on the Kwanza River where he died of mysterious circumstances.

Njinga Mbandi became queen, just as her nurse and her father had imagined many years before.

Queen Njinga was a strong ruler. She worked hard to keep her people safe and free. She defended them from the Portuguese and from all who threatened them.

In time, however, threats against the Ndongo became too great for the people. The land was no longer safe. *Ngola* Njinga fought to conquer the Kingdom of Matamba and moved her people there. Now she was queen of two united kingdoms.

Despite the difficulties she faced, Njinga Mbandi remained queen for many years. Her brother was wrong. Njinga was not "just a girl." She was a smart ruler, a gifted queen, and a brave warrior. To this very day, she is remembered as the determined and courageous Queen Njinga of Ndongo and Matamba.

THE NDONGO AND MATAMBA KINGDOMS IN ANGOLA, AFRICA

- Angola is the seventh-largest country in Africa. Africa is a continent. The world contains seven continents.

- The kingdom of Ndongo was located in what is now called Angola. The kingdom of Matamba was located in what is now called the Democratic Republic of Congo.

- The language spoken by the Ndongo people was **Kimbundu**. This is the language used for some phrases in this story!

- Angola's name comes from the Ndongo people's word for king: *Ngola*.

- The Portuguese were the first Europeans to come to Angola. The Portuguese explorer, Diogo Cao, arrived in 1484.

It was not easy to be a ruler over Ndongo. The kingdom faced multiple problems.

While some Portuguese wanted to help Ndongo's people, others (including some among the government) wanted to take their land and make them slaves.

The Kingdom of Kongo threatened to take over Ndongo and demanded riches in return for safety and peace. Kongo also took slaves from neighboring kingdoms; some they kept, and others were sold to the Portuguese.

The Imbangala were a warrior group that threatened to topple other kingdoms and set up their own. Njinga married their chief because she wanted to achieve peace with the group. The Imbangala helped Njinga ascend to power in Matamba but later betrayed her, attacking Matamba.

After Njinga's death, Portugal did finally take over Angola, and Angola did not again win its independence until many years later.

Today, Angola is an important country and economy in Africa. Many of the world's diamonds come from Angola, and Angola is also a big oil producer.

NJINGA OF NDONGO AND MATAMBA

- Njinga was born around the year 1581 and died around 1663. She lived for about 82 years.

- The name Njinga is derived from the Kimbundu verb *kujinga*, meaning "to twist or turn."

- During Njinga's life, her land and people faced being taken over by Europeans, especially Portuguese. Njinga's leadership allowed Angola to avoid such conquests during her lifetime.

- Njinga became Queen of Ndongo in 1623, at about age 42.

- As queen, Njinga promptly declared to the world that Angola was a free and independent country.

- Sometime after Njinga became queen, the Portuguese broke the agreement that they had made with her. They attacked Ndongo, forcing Njinga to escape (as she had done early in her brother's reign) to Matamba.

- Njinga married the chief of the warrior group Imbangala. (In many cultures throughout history, marriage was often used to create political partnerships.) Njinga was able to use the Imbangala warriors to conquer Matamba and become queen.

But the Imbangala later abandoned their loyalty to Njinga and attacked Matamba, and Njinga had to go into hiding (exile).

Since so many remained loyal to her, Njinga was able to lead even from exile. She commanded warriors in battle against the Portuguese. At the same time, she made friends with the Dutch (other European people present in Africa) to persuade them in her cause against Portugal. She demonstrated exceptional abilities both militarily and politically.

Queen Njinga Mbande is known by many different names, including both Kimbundu and Portuguese names, alternate spellings, and various honorifics. Common spellings found in Portuguese and English sources include Nzinga, Nzingha, Njinga, and Njingha. In colonial documentation, including her own manuscripts, her name was also spelled Jinga, Ginga, Zinga, Zingua, Zhinga, and Singa. She was also known by her Christian name, Ana de Sousa.

In a significant amount of text, Njinga's name is spelled as Nzinga. The confusion regarding the spelling of Queen Njinga's name comes from the way the letters in the Kimbundu language are pronounced. In Kimbundu, her name is spelled Njinga Mbandi.

The "j" is a "soft j" (pronounced *zh*) similar to the sounds used in the words "Ta**j**" or "mea**s**ure." The adjacent "n" is silent.

In Portuguese, she was known as Rainha Nzinga/Zinga/Ginga (Queen Nzingha).

SOUTHWEST AFRICA AND ANGOLA

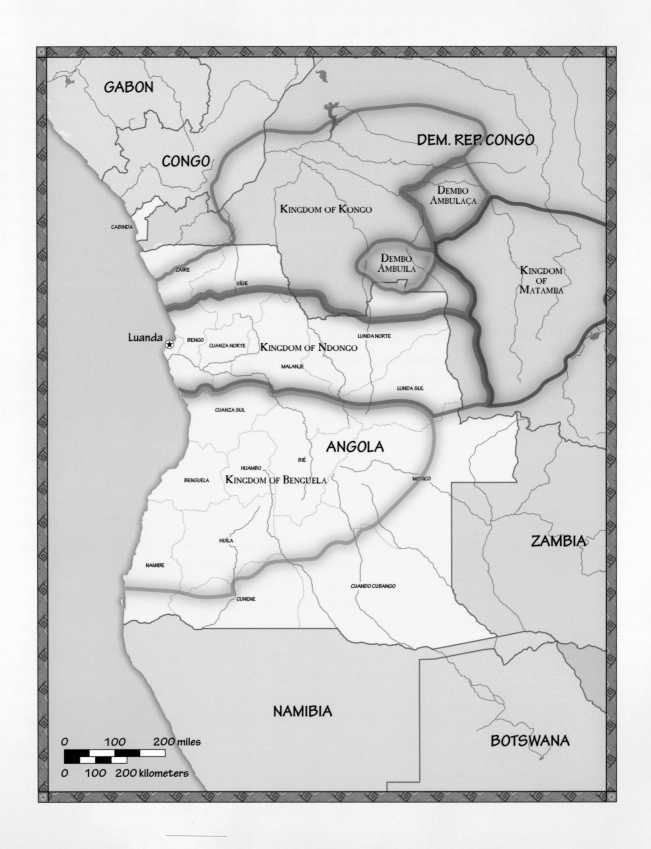

GABON

CONGO

DEM. REP. CONGO

CABINDA

Dembo
Ambulaça

ZAIRE

UÍGE

KINGDOM OF KONGO

Dembo
Ambuila

KINGDOM
OF
MATAMBA

Luanda

BENGO

CUANZA NORTE

LUNDA NORTE

KINGDOM OF NDONGO

MALANJE

LUNDA SUL

CUANZA SUL

ANGOLA

BIÉ

MOXICO

HUAMBO

BENGUELA

KINGDOM OF BENGUELA

ZAMBIA

HUÍLA

NAMIBE

CUANDO CUBANGO

CUNENE

NAMIBIA

BOTSWANA

0   100   200 miles

0   100   200 kilometers

ABOUT THE AUTHOR

Ekiuwa Aire was born and raised in Benin City, Edo, Nigeria. She moved to England when she was nine and it was here, away from all she had grown up with, that she discovered her passion for writing. Ekiuwa co-wrote her first book while finishing high school and continued developing her craft while earning a Bachelor of Science in Economics and a Master of Business Administration. She is passionate about African history and incorporates the richness of many cultures into her books. Now a mother living in Canada, Ekiuwa hopes that her books will help kids develop an appreciation for African history, and to value the wisdom and pride that will come from this knowledge.

ABOUT THE ILLUSTRATOR

Natalia Popova studied at Moscow State University where her interest in visual arts and illustration was born. After graduation, she landed a corporate job with an international media agency in Moscow. While in this management role, Natalia continued to work hard on her drawing skills. As her abilities improved, more clients requested her services. She eventually quit her management role and became a full-time freelance artist. She specializes in character designs, commercials, and book illustrations. Years ago, she moved to a new home close to the ocean in Bali.